# Books by Rosemary Rosedale

My Dog Munye

Munye Matters

# MY DOG MUNYE
## A TRUE STORY

Rosemary Rosedale

My Dog Munye

Rosemary Rosedale

© 2025 Cosmos Press

ISBN 978-0-9935332-9-7

The right of the author to be identified as the author of this work has been asserted in accordance with the Copyright, Designs and Patents Act 1988.

Photography copyright the author

All rights reserved.

No part of this publication may be reproduced, stored in a retrieval system, or transmitted, in any form or by any means, electronic, mechanical, photocopying, recording or otherwise, without the prior permission of the copyright owners.

COSMOS PRESS

*For Danny*

*Munye's biggest fan*

# Contents

| | |
|---|---|
| Winning the Battle | 9 |
| Back to the Beginning | 15 |
| Munye's older Brother | 21 |
| Munye's first Month | 23 |
| Mobile, Messy and Mischief | 29 |
| Mischief | 33 |
| Teenage Times | 41 |
| Wild Walks | 47 |
| Full Circle | 53 |
| Munye and Friends | 57 |
| About King Charles Spaniels | 58 |

# Winning the Battle

It was a cold, sunny Monday morning. Snow had fallen during the night and everything was white.

I was walking to school with my Dad. He kept jerking the lead as our family dog, Sawubona, (Sabbie for short), stopped every few steps to have a good sniff. Sabbie is always sniffing and wagging her tail.

"Come on, Sabbie," Dad would say, "We haven't got all day. Danny has got to get to school."

My mind wasn't on school at all. For the very first time Munye, Sabbie's one and only puppy, was trotting along with us on a lead. And I was holding the lead. I felt so proud.

Every now and then one of my school friends would pass us then stop and say "Danny is that your puppy? Gee, you're so lucky!"

*YES! I am*, I thought.

Dad had been silent. Suddenly he said rather sternly "Danny you know Munye is not your puppy. He will be sold." My heart sank. I thought of the fun we'd had with the dogs in the garden before leaving for school. It was the first time Munye had seen snow.

He just loved it! He was such a fun puppy. He was always game for anything and much more lively than Sabbie too. How could Dad want to sell him?

My heart sank lower – into the very bottom of my boots, but only for a moment. This can't happen, I thought. Munye is such a special puppy. Munye is going to be mine.

Mum had told me that Dad was determined to sell Munye but she and I wanted to keep him and so did my brother. What could I do? There must be a way of getting Dad to agree.

"It's up to you," Mum had said a few days ago. "If you really want to keep Munye you will have to persuade Dad. But remember Munye will be your responsibility. You will have to look after him. You will walk him, brush him, feed him, train him, and clean up the mess he makes."

Now I was up against it. I had to work on Dad and work fast. This was my moment. I chose my words carefully.

"Dad, please can we keep Munye?"

"NO," replied Dad.

"Please, Daddy, please. I will look after him. I promise."

"NO. I said no and I mean no," he said. "Munye has

got to go and go soon. We are not having two dogs in the family. We've already got two boys and two cats. One dog is enough!"

*Gulp! Oh no! This can't happen*, I thought. *What can I do? What can I say?*

"Dad," I said, putting on my most persuasive voice, "Dad if you let me keep Munye, I'll give you Zulu." (Zulu is a tortoiseshell cat who belonged to me.) It is no secret that Dad really likes cats. I thought I saw him soften – just a little. Then his face clouded over and he said in almost a shout "NO, Danny, NO."

We had reached the school gates and stood there. Streams of kids were flooding past us. This was the moment to hold my tongue I thought. So I did. I looked longingly over my shoulder at Dad walking up the hill with the two dogs.

It was hard to concentrate on lessons. I had to find a way of keeping Munye. I'd never loved an animal quite so much. Sabbie and Munye belonged to each other.

Sabbie and Munye looked good together even when curled up asleep.

Besides Munye wouldn't be happy anywhere else.

It wasn't fair.

The day dragged on. Eventually the end of school bell rang. I was ready to go and left quickly – but walked home the long way. I needed time to think. I came to the conclusion that it would be best to say nothing more about Munye. I would just hope and pray that Dad would give in.

I had a lot of fun with Munye that afternoon in the garden. Then I took him and Sabbie for a walk around the block.

We had a delicious dinner that night. Everyone had something to tell about the happenings of the day. Everyone seemed happy – except me.

Suddenly Dad banged his spoon on the table. "I have an announcement to make," he said. This was unusual so we all sat up straight and listened.

"I've decided Munye can stay! But there are two conditions. First, Zulu is mine from this day on. Secondly, Munye belongs to Danny and Danny must look after him."

I yelled "Whoopee!" and gave Dad a great big hug, and another. At last, I thought, Munye is no longer a shadow on my mind,

### Munye is mine!

I promised to look after Munye – walk Munye,

brush Munye, clean any mess he made and anything else. I was so happy – so happy!

Munye seemed to know. Suddenly he bounced up and down and then took a flying leap over Sabbie. Then he grabbed a paper serviette that had fallen on the floor and tore it to shreds.

The mess had begun! I had to clear it up! But Munye was worth it.

*Sabbie, Zulu and Munye (about 10 weeks old)*

When it was bedtime I looked around for Munye. Where was he? After a big hunt I finally checked his basket. There he was, as he had often been before, snuggled up with his mother, and Zulu. I guess they had a lot to talk about!

# Back to the Beginning

IT WAS 1999 and the last Saturday of the summer holidays. Everyone was talking about how exciting it would be in the New Millennium. I thought it would look funny writing 2000 for the year.

At that point I was much more interested in Sabbie. She was looking fat and wobbling about uncomfortably. She seemed hot and tired and was panting. Any day now she would have her first litter of puppies.

It all began nine weeks before when Sabbie went to stay in Reading with a dog called Matthew. Like Sabbie, Matthew is a pedigree King Charles spaniel. As they are both tricolour (mainly white with some black and tan colouring) we knew the puppies would be tricolour too. I just couldn't wait to see them.

A month after Sabbie had been with Matthew we took her to see the vet. He examined her and said he could feel 4 embryos. We were all very excited.

The vet warned us not to get too excited until we actually saw the puppies. He explained that sometimes, for example if there were problems for Sabbie before the puppies were born, she might re-absorb some or all of them. That was odd, I thought. I didn't believe him.

Three weeks before Sabbie's puppies were due when we were out walking we kept coming across Muffins. Muffins was a mongrel dog who definitely did not like Sabbie. At every opportunity Muffins would give a deep growl, rush for Sabbie and try to bite her. Once by an ear, her tail, or worst of all, by her throat. Sabbie was terrified. A week before Sabbie's puppies were due we decided to keep Sabbie inside our own garden. She was much happier. I was looking forward so much to having four puppies. I'd forgotten what the vet said.

It was the first Saturday in September. Sabbie was very restless. She was rushing from one side of the garden to the other and then into the house. Then back into the garden again. She kept digging holes and grunting. Dad said she was trying to reach her boyfriend in Australia. Mum replied that was nonsense and that the puppies must be coming soon. Mum went in to telephone the vet to tell him how Sabbie was.

Mum soon came back and took Sabbie inside. I'm not sure how long she was there because my brother and I were fooling about in the tree at the end of the garden. That tree always gives us lots of fun. Earlier we had built a tree house, a swing and a rope slide. But the tree house wasn't very safe and one-day it collapsed and I fell out and hurt myself.

After some time Mum came out. Her face seemed to say something both sad and glad. "Listen very carefully, I will say this only once," she said with a twinkle in her eye as she spoke to us brothers. "Sabbie has started having her puppies. So far we've got one puppy."

"Gee Ma, can we see it?" we said together. "Jinks personally!" we shouted in chorus. "I want to hold it first," I said very loudly.

"Wait," said Mum, "you haven't asked whether it is a boy or a girl."

"Go on then, tell us, please."

"It's a boy!" she announced. "The dogs are in the study. Come with me. But you must not touch the puppy or Sawubona may reject it. Be quiet – she could be fierce."

To be on the safe side we peeped through the open window. At first it was hard to see, as it was dark after being in the sunshine. No one spoke.

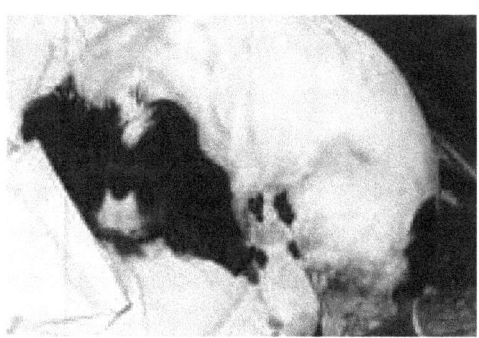

Then we heard a tiny squeak like a mouse.

Something minute moved slightly half buried in Sabbie's fur. It was the size of a medium pork sausage but unlike a sausage it was white splattered with a little black. It was so cute.

Several hours went by but no more puppies arrived. As we were expecting 4 puppies Mum decided to call the vet in case something was going wrong for Sabbie. I went with Mum and was surprised when the vet said there were no more puppies. I was extra sad because we had agreed not to keep a boy dog. This meant he could only stay with us for about eight weeks.

"Oh well, I will have fun with him as long and as I can," I thought.

That night Mum took the dogs to her and Dad's bedroom. "Oh no! I want to sleep," said Dad, and went to make his bed downstairs.

My brother crept in to help Mum in case of any problems. They did not get much sleep as the puppy kept squeaking all night and kept losing his mother. Mum kept moving him back. She was worried he might die of cold so she kept filling a hot water bottle, covering it with an old towel and putting it under the dogs.

The next important step was to give the puppy a name. We had thought of many names before it was born but now none of them seemed to suit him. So for the night we called him Puppy. But in the morning we were happy. The puppy was alive and suckling well. And so we got together to

### BRAINSTORM!

At last we agreed that an only-child-puppy must be called Munye – a Zulu word that means one.

# Munye's older Brother

THIS CHAPTER HEADING sounds like a riddle! How come Munye has an older brother if Munye is an only-child-dog? The answer is this. Munye is an only-child-dog. He had an older brother but that brother, although born half an hour before Munye, never breathed, so never lived.

After Mum had shown us the live puppy she brought out the little dead Big Brother on some newspaper. I was so sad and cried when no one was looking.

I took the bundle from her and walked slowly to the bench at the bottom of the garden. There I sat and gazed at Big Brother. What a cool dog he was. His head marking was similar to that of Sabbie. What was unique was the cloak he was wearing like an old lady wears! He was perfectly formed but he wasn't breathing.

I turned him over and stroked his side again and again hoping that this would bring him to life. I had heard the vet say that sometimes a still born puppy comes to life when stroked firmly along its rib cage But no, not this time.

I sat on the swing bench and looked and looked at him. My brother looked too. We didn't say anything.

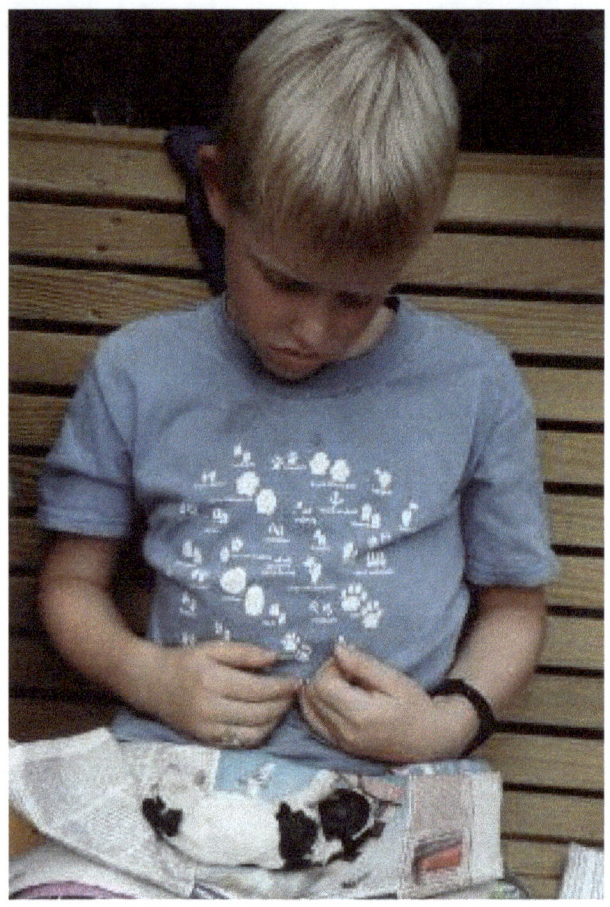

After a long time we wrapped him up. I dug a hole behind the Red-tree. We said "goodbye" and together we buried him.

# Munye's first Month

MUNYE WAS BORN on 4 September 2000. For the first month of his life he spent his time sleeping, eating and growing. I couldn't believe how quickly he grew.

As Munye was the only puppy, Sabbie had far more milk than he needed. And so he sucked and sucked and grew fatter and fatter. I thought he was going to pop like a balloon when you blow too much air into it!

After a week we were allowed to pick Munye up. He usually snuggled down happily. It was hard to tell whether he was asleep or not as he never opened his eyes.

This was normal. All puppies are born blind and do not see for about 10 days. I used to wonder if he recognised any of us. I think he did through his sense of smell.

*Munye – one week old*

From the very beginning Munye was energetic – especially about his food (like me!). Just look at him in this picture and you will see what I mean. I called him the gymnast, or my acrobat!

*The Acrobat*

After a good long feed Munye would lie back with a look of satisfaction. I think he must have been dreaming about the next feed. Maybe he tried to imagine what the world would be like when he could see.

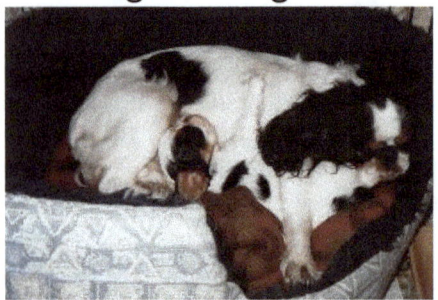
*The satisfied customer*

Munye was so tiny. He looked even tinier when Dad held him. One of his hands made a comfortable bed for our puppy!

Dad seemed to like little Munye.

Sabbie was always on guard when someone was holding him... Whenever anyone else tried to touch Munye she looked worried and went onto:

**Red Alert.**

If one of the cats came near she would send them off in a hurry. I kept my distance!

But sometimes it was my turn to hold Munye and Sabbie didn't seem to mind.

*Munye, Sabbie and Dad*

**Munye grew like grass.**

***The day he was born*** the vet checked him out. "You have a perfect puppy," he said. "He weighs 6 oz. He will grow very quickly. He will be ready to leave you for a new home when he is 8 to 10 weeks old."

Oh NO I thought. This puppy is going to stay with us. He was so cute. Besides, Sabbie would be lonely. I'd have to work on Dad.

I didn't want Munye to grow too quickly but I was looking forward to the day he could run about.

**At one week** we weighed him on our kitchen scales. He was 9 oz. He had put on half his birth-weight in 7 days.

**At two weeks** he was nearly 3 times his birth weight.

**At three weeks** he was 24 oz – 4 times his birth weight! By then we thought it was time to 'go-metric' so we weighed him in grams too – almost 700 Gms.

One week old

Here he is in the same kitchen scale *at seven weeks*.

This was the big surprise. Can you believe it? He was about 1100 grams. In old measures this is 39 oz. He was a whopper at about 6 ½ times his birth weight. Why don't you check to see if I am right!

Seven weeks old

26

One day I noticed Sabbie starting to teach Munye manners!

*Now you listen to me, young man!*

I caught her talking to him in a whisper. I think I know what she was saying.

He must have been getting a telling off! Munye was definitely giving a lot of backchat and Sabbie was looking very stern and disapproving.

After they'd had it out for a while they both fell asleep, exhausted by the stress of the battle. Sabbie was snoring - as usual. Munye looked defeated!

*No, I won't. I don't want to!*

# Mobile, Messy and Mischief

MUNYE'S EYES WERE big and wide open. As expected they had started opening on about day ten. Ever since then he'd seemed frustrated. He kept looking around staring intently at something. A loud squeal, sigh or grunt would follow.

Then, one day he took off and headed straight for the food!

*Food, food, glorious food!*

He was a bit wobbly at first but soon became confident.

Sabbie watched his every move. It did not take her long before she started her motherly instruction! I'm sure she was saying "Do this. Don't do that. Mind this. Watch that!" All parents do.

As I watched them I'm sure I heard Sabbie go on about toilet training. I tried to hear what she was saying. I think I got it.

*Munye, you do understand this is Dad's best carpet?*

*Yes, Mamma*

Munye couldn't wait to get away! He didn't like being told what to do. So as soon as Sabbie finished her speech he was off exploring. Any whiff of food moved him along even faster.

*So many interesting smells!*

Munye is definitely intelligent.

Who else would read the paper when less than two months old?

There wasn't much he would not try! But sometimes he went a little too far. It was not long before he was caught out!

*Oh no, Munye, you haven't! Not on the RED carpet!*

Sabbie was patient but persistent in her training.

I was sure Sabbie forgave Munye and told him to keep trying.

That's what parents do.

Munye looked so innocent that nobody could be cross with him for very long – not even Dad.

Dad would capture him when he was up to no good and pin him down. Eventually Munye would wriggle free. I'm sure he was already thinking up the next bit of mischief.

# Mischief

MUNYE BECAME MORE and more handsome. Light brown hair grew round his mouth and under his ears. He looked so innocent and cute when he was asleep. You wouldn't believe how naughty he could be and how mercilessly he teased his mother.

*Bliss!*

They had a games routine. Sabbie would be, or pretend to be asleep. Munye whined. When there was no response he'd grab Sabbie by an ear, her tail or anywhere else and TUG.

When Sabbie had had enough her eyes lit up like fire and Munye got told off! He always had something to say.

*Don't be cross Mamma, It was all in fun!*

33

Sabbie was most reasonable and seemed to understand.

*I like fun too. But remember sometimes I need to sleep. Also, you are too rough. Find someone your own age to bully, will you!*

Munye always had a BUT...

*But Mamma, there are no other puppies to play with. The cats and people are much bigger than me.*

*But I know the answer. You, Mamma should have some more puppies... I'd love a brother or sister or both.*

Sabbie didn't look impressed. She was only just recovering from Munye's arrival. She ignored his comment. After a while she suggested Munye might like a little drink! He thought this was a very good idea and immediately latched on. And

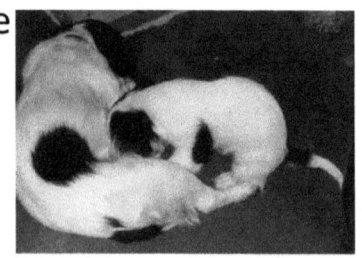

so there was peace, peace surrounded by the sounds of contented sucking.

All was so quiet you could have heard a pin drop until Munye stirred.

Mischief peeped over the top of his mother. Peace was threatened. I read his thoughts!

*What next?*

Slowly, Munye unwound himself from Sabbie and wandered off leaving her sleeping. He sniffed and snuffled around for a bit and then sat down with his eyes fixed on something. There was a glint of delight in his eyes.

Munye wasn't one for sitting around for very long. He had to be occupied. He liked a challenge. If nobody set him one he'd invent one himself.

*What is that over there? YES! There is someone I know well at the other end of it.*

*I can smell it from here. I wonder where it's been today? Now that's a very interesting smell. I must go and investigate.*

Munye trotted over to the object he'd been staring at and began to sniff vigorously.

"Hey Mum!" I whispered. "Get your camera ready. I think Munye is about to do something interesting." Fortunately Mum could reach the camera without moving. And this is what we saw.

*Sniff, sniff, sniff, sniff. I've not smelt anything like this before. Where has it been? What is it?*

*What about the rest of this thing? Let me explore and find out.*

*Ah ha! This is the thing I've seen her tie lots of times. I wonder if I can undo it without her knowing.*

It did not take Munye long to completely destroy mums shoelace-tying work. What he did not know was that his monkey business was being captured on camera as evidence!

*Got it! I am pulling but why won't it undo?*

*Oh, that's better. I've found the end. Now all I have to do is TUG.*

Munye had done it! It had taken him 5 minutes and 42 seconds to untie a shoelace for the first time. I'd timed him using my watch. What a star! I usually took longer to untie mine especially when they were knotty.

*Yippee! This is a first, I knew I could do it. Ha ha! Just you wait...*

And I got into trouble! Mum only laughed at Munye. It's not fair!

Next, Munye decided to go for unattached objects like my slipper.

*Cool! This belongs to the bullyboy. His mum tells him not to be rough.*

*I'll get my own back! He's not supposed to leave his slippers lying around.*

I couldn't believe Munye was only 2 months and 4 days old. He was bright and full of ideas. I eyed him carefully.

Fortunately I realised what he was up to and rescued my slipper in time.

*I wonder if I can destroy this.*

Now that Munye had started

chewing things he tried chewing everything he could see. He even tried chewing Dad's watch. But Dad was not amused and shouted at him.

*Hey you little blighter! STOP IT!*

To try and keep the peace Mum and I bought him his own slipper and a hard ring. He seemed to like them both, especially the ring. I think he was teething.

For a while he seemed content.

However Munye didn't look after his toys very well and they soon got lost. Then he was on the hunt again for new things to amuse him.

My dad said this was just like my brother and me. Perhaps he was right.

When Munye couldn't find anything better to do he would pester his Mamma. He'd go on and on until she took some notice of him and played his games with him. I think dogs are like us humans!

Munye was always enthusiastic. He tore around endlessly and then collapsed and slept for hours. He loved curling up with Sabbie, Zulu, Ntombi or my brother (a pre-teen) who also spends a lot of time asleep.

I'll let Munye have the last word in this chapter!

*Why is everybody always picking on me!*

# Teenage Times

TEENAGE TIMES ARE marked by "self-discovery". At least that is what Mum says. We decided Munye must be a teenager when we caught him trying to lick his image in the mirror.

I remember the first time he saw himself in the mirror. He got a fright and barked at the 'other' dog! Later, when he was used to the mirror, he spent hours looking at himself.

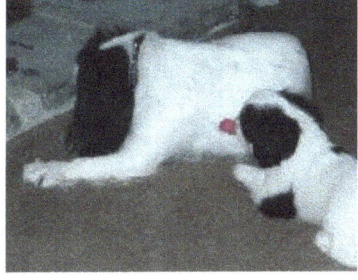

He also discovered his long tongue and started licking everything including the carpet, our shoes, and even the end of my nose! Sabbie had never looked so clean!

Munye hated being bathed by us but sometimes it was necessary!

*How undignified!*

He always tried to get out of it if he could. But his hiding places were always discovered! He looked really odd when he was wet and cringed when we laughed at him.

Teen times bring more freedom. Munye was delighted that he could now go out in the garden. He especially liked chasing the autumn leaves and playing

*This is such fun. Mamma, you are fun too!*

games with whoever was around. Sabbie became his main playmate. She was much more energetic and enjoyed a good game

Munye loved to tease Sabbie. He would find something like an old carrot, put in his mouth and run up to her with a little growl. Then he ran away and back again until she chased him.

They were so funny.

Munye liked to win. He often had a tussle with Sabbie but was always very unhappy when he lost. This time it was over a huge bone our butcher had sent him. He had no intention of losing this battle. The reward was too big.

*This is the chewiest thing I've ever eaten! I'll bury it when I've had enough so Mamma can't get it.*

Growing up brings responsibilities, as Munye was to discover. No longer could he sleep in the warmth of the main house. Instead he was given the job of being a guard dog. This meant that his 'box' was, from then on, in the conservatory near to the back door. He did the job very well as he was quick to bark at the slightest sound. Usually it was at one of the cats coming

through the cat flap. No burglars got in with him around!

Munye felt important in his guard-dog role. But he was a bit cold and lonely at times especially when Sabbie was somewhere else. So he thought up a plan. When nobody was looking, he sneaked into my bedroom and raided my cuddly toys.

The first thing Mum and I knew about it was when Munye slid past with Miss Piggy in his mouth. He headed straight for his box.

Sadly it was Miss Piggy who was often lonely and pink with cold while Munye was out and about.

# Wild Walks

THE COLD, SNOWY February days were over. Munye was mine and I was happy. He was over 6 months old. In dog-terms he was a late teenager fast becoming a young adult.

Munye, didn't like it at first, but learnt to walk on a lead. He soon saw the advantages - longer and better walks like a special spot along the river.

Munye saw a new side to his Mamma. He avoided the mud puddles but Sabbie wallowed in them. He thought this was disgusting and could not believe this dirty dog was his Mamma.

Back home they both had a bath though Munye was clean. It wasn't fair! He hated bathing.

It helped a bit that they were wrapped up and allowed to read the newspaper over dinner!

*Model mother?*

One day a new excitement drove down the street and parked outside the front door - Dad's new car. Munye and Sabbie were allowed to ride in it. This meant more interesting walks further from home. They were chuffed.

Sometimes Munye was taken out on his own on longer walks in the country. It gave him a chance to see how fast he could run. He was faster than me no matter how hard I tried. He liked to stop and admire the view.

When we got back home Munye would tell Sabbie all about his adventures. Then they would tear off round the garden and play tag or hide and seek.

There were so many walks. After a big storm we came across a tree that had been uprooted

After school we had fun on the playing field. My school is in woods on a rabbit filled hillside.

49

One day Mum and I decided to take Munye on his first bike ride. We wanted to train him to run alongside a bike, on a lead. First we had to get him to the fields. So, Mum

*Munye! What are you doing in there?*

decided to carry him in her rucksack. Sabbie looked alarmed!

*Mamma, it's OK. I'll tell you all about it. Bye byeeee!*

Sabbie looked even more worried as Mum put on the rucksack and headed outside.

The bike ride was cool but Munye almost tangled with the wheels!

At bedtime Sabbie heard the whole story. She looked somewhat worried as Mums do. But it was Ntombi, who had come to listen, who looked really startled.

When Munye was 11 months we took the dogs with us on holiday. We stayed in Bridge, a country village, near Canterbury.

*Walks in all directions!*

And lots of variety: orchards, vineyards, long grass,

poppies, wheat fields, woodlands, flax fields, fox holes and the sea. It was thirsty work.

My brother had fun with Munye in the fields.

Near the end of our holiday we went to a horse and dog show. I discovered I could enter Munye in two sections, so I did. It was a bit scary, as I had to show him. But Munye was born a star. He wasn't afraid but full of fun. In both classes he won a prize! He wasn't even a year old. I was so proud of him. Munye and I were the youngest.

*Some competitors in Most Handsome dog class*

Munye's biggest ordeal ever came at the end of the holidays. Mum and Dad were at a beach with Munye. Sabbie stayed at home as she was very tired. My brother and I were at a camp. Mum thought it time Munye learnt to swim. So, keeping his lead on, she carried him into the sea and put him gently into the water. No problem! He swam! Mum says he looked dead scared. She thinks he was dreaming of dry land!

# Full Circle

THE DAY CAME to go home. Munye ran round in excited circles. He always ran circles round us when we were going anywhere especially if he heard the word 'walk'.

Sabbie was looking large and moved very slowly. She was expecting puppies – 4 as far as the vet could tell. In fact the puppies were due on Munye's birthday. Full circle?

Munye was a handsome, slim line young adult. He had missed having fun with Sabbie because she was so heavy with puppies and no longer energetic. I think he was looking forward to having brothers and sisters.

Meanwhile, for the journey home he chose his favourite seat – Mum's lap in the front – so he could look out of the window.

Now it sometimes

happens that when we get what we have been wanting so very badly, we don't want it anymore. This is what happened to Munye.

Two weeks after we got home, and two days early, Sabbie had 4 puppies. Full circle! Poor Munye! Instead of playmates he was more alone than he had ever been in his life. He no longer had his  Mamma to curl up to as she looked after her new litter all day and all night. He wasn't even allowed to see his brothers and sisters.

Munye had dreamt of fun with the new puppies. Instead, everyone shouted at him to stay out of the way. He spent a lot of time sleeping at the bottom of the garden, alone, and lonely. Until then he had been the centre of attention. Worst of all we had forgotten his first birthday.

But Munye is a STAR! He is not one to feel sorry for himself for long. He soon found other things to do and new 'toys' to play with.

I could write much more about my dog Munye. Books and books! But what I have written will give you a flavour of his character. Maybe one day I will introduce you to his brothers and sisters and tell you how they all get along!

# Munye and Friends
## Their names and meanings

**Zulu** is a language (with lots of clicks) spoken by the **Zulu people** who mainly live in South Africa. Our animals all have Zulu names.

### Zulu

A Zulu coloured cat – a tortoiseshell female. Zulu, born in 1997, has a soft, silent walk and very soft purr. She was mine but now she belongs to Dad.

### Ntombi

A tortoiseshell female cat that wears a large white bib! She is Zulu's twin sister, born in 1997. Ntombi means "girl". Ntombi walks noisily, purrs loudly, and belongs to my brother. These two are 'alley-cats'.

### Sawubona

A pedigree King Charles spaniel. Sawubona means "Hello" said in a friendly way. Sawubona is shy and loyal to all the family. She was born in January 1997 and was our first pet. Sabbie belongs to Mum.

### Munye

A pedigree King Charles spaniel. Munye means "One" - the only pup from Sawubona's first litter. Born in 1999, he is intelligent, energetic, and excitable (like me). He likes everyone and is the best dog in the whole world. Munye is mine.

## About King Charles Spaniels

Mystery! Nobody knows exactly when the King Charles Spaniel breed was started. But, the first written reference to the breed in England is around 1570.

There are some funny stories.

Queen Elizabeth I called these little dogs 'Comforters' or 'Gentle Spaniels'. Ladies of The Court kept them under their voluminous skirts close to the feet and body! In 1587 someone wrote that a tiny blood soaked spaniel was found under the skirts of Mary Queen of Scots, after she was executed. It was taken away and washed. During the reigns of King Charles I and King Charles II, from 1625 to 1685, these little dogs became very popular. King Charles II named them after himself. His palace was full of them and the King was often seen walking in St. James' park followed by several of his dogs. Today, given half a chance, Charlies (their nickname) will dive under bedclothes, snuggle close to the occupant, and start snoring!

**Charlies come in four colours.**

**Black and Tan** (glossy black with mahogany and tan markings)

**Tricolour** (pearly white with black patches) and bright tan markings on cheeks, above eyes etc.

**Blenheim** (white with chestnut-red patches)

**Ruby** (a rich chestnut-red 'whole colour').

Adults weigh 6 to 12 pounds (about 2.7 to 5.4 Kgs.). Charlies have a large domed head, a stubby black nose, long ears and the most beautiful large, sad and expressive eyes. They are gentle, fun loving, loyal, friendly and don't bite or bark very much! They keep themselves clean.

Sadly some end up in rescue homes when their owners die or don't want them.

**Do you?**

If you want to know more read:

The King Charles Spaniel;
by M. Joyce Birchall 1987;
ISBN 0707106125

www.ingramcontent.com/pod-product-compliance
Lightning Source LLC
Chambersburg PA
CBHW042301030526
44119CB00066B/841